Meerkats at Work

Written by Nancy O'Connor

Flying Start
to Literacy®

Contents

Introduction

Meerkats are small mammals. They live
in the desert in Africa.

Meerkats live in large groups called mobs.
Each mob is made up of several families that
live together in a burrow under the ground.

There can be as many as 50 meerkats
in one mob.

The mob has important jobs to do – hunting for food, protecting the mob and babysitting. Every meerkat in the mob, except the youngest pups, takes turns to do these jobs.

Chapter 1:
Hunting for food

Meerkats dig in the sand to find food. They eat mostly insects. They also eat lizards, worms and spiders. Sometimes they even eat scorpions.

Meerkats have large front paws to help them dig. They have an excellent sense of smell and can smell insects under the sand. They spend most of the day hunting for food.

Meerfact

Every meerkat has a different pattern of stripes across its back. No two are alike.

Feeding the mob

Each meerkat finds its own food. The pups cannot find food so all the meerkats share their food with the pups.

Meerfact

Meerkats can close their ears when they dig in the sand to find food. This stops sand from getting in their ears.

When older meerkats find a tasty bug, they give it to the pups. Usually, the pup that begs the loudest gets the most food.

Chapter 2:

Keeping safe

When meerkats hunt for food, they cannot see predators, such as snakes, eagles and jackals. So, while the mob is hunting, the meerkats take turns to watch out for predators.

Guard duty

When a meerkat is on guard duty, it climbs up onto high ground. It stands up on its two hind legs and watches for predators while the rest of the mob hunts for food.

Meerfact

A meerkat uses its tail to balance when it stands on its two hind legs.

Danger calls

When a predator comes near, the meerkat on guard duty makes calls to warn the others of danger. The calls get louder as the predator comes closer. Meerkats have different calls for different kinds of predators.

When the mob hears a danger call, it knows which predator is close by. The meerkats run to safety.

Meerkats have secret tunnels called boltholes where they hide until the predator leaves. Sometimes, they stir up the dust to hide the bolthole.

Meerfact

Birds called drongos can mimic meerkat danger calls. When a drongo mimics a danger call, the meerkats run and hide. The drongo then eats the food the meerkats have left behind!

Chapter 3:
Protecting their home

Meerkats are brave animals. Sometimes the members of one mob join together to fight off another mob or another animal that wants to live in their burrow.

Meerkats can make themselves look bigger by standing together. They stand on all four legs and arch their backs.

Fighting a mob

Often mobs live close to each other. If a neighbouring meerkat mob tries to take over another mob's territory, the large meerkat family will fight to chase them away.

Fighting home invaders

Some animals such as the deadly yellow cobra will try to make a home in the meerkats' burrow. When this happens, the mob gathers at the entrance and stands up tall. Then they fight!

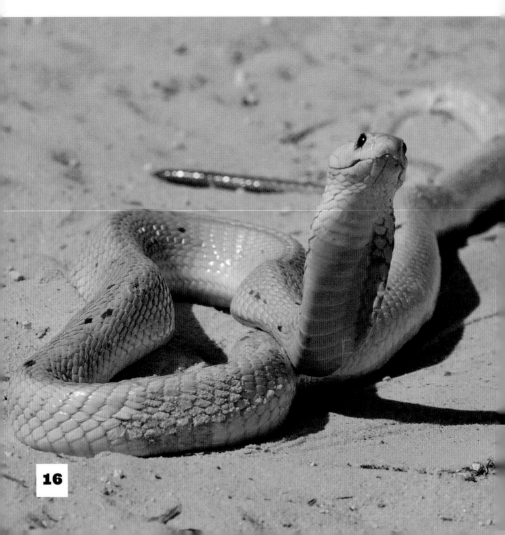

They wave their tails in the air to confuse the snake. They hiss, nip and growl until the deadly yellow cobra gives up and slithers away.

Chapter 4:
Babysitting

Meerkats take turns to look after the pups in the mob.

Meerkat pups love to play and groom each other. They also like to explore. It is a big job to keep the meerkat pups safe and out of the tall grass where predators such as jackals often hide.

Meerfact

When a baby meerkat is born, its eyes are closed. Its eyes open when it is two weeks old.

Feeding the pups

Like all mammals, meerkat pups drink milk from their mother when they are first born.

When meerkat pups are about one month old, older meerkats teach them how to hunt for food. They show the pups the best places to dig.

Eating poisonous animals

Sometimes, meerkats eat poisonous animals such as scorpions. They have to teach the pups how to eat scorpions safely.

First, an older meerkat catches a scorpion and bites off its stinger. Then it gives the live scorpion to the pups. The pups can practise killing a scorpion without getting hurt by the poisonous tail.

Before an adult meerkat eats a scorpion, it drags it through the sand to rub off the poison.

Conclusion

During the day, meerkats work together to keep the mob safe in the African desert.

At night, the meerkats curl up in their warm burrow. They know that they have worked together to keep their big family safe for another day.

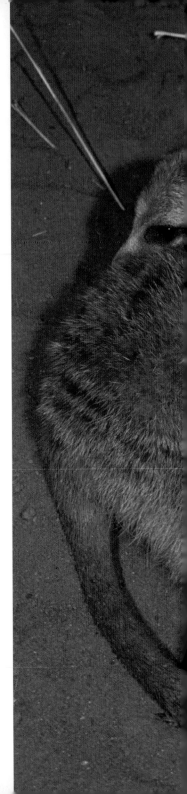

Glossary

bolthole   When meerkats are in danger from predators, they run and hide in special tunnels that have a wide opening.   These tunnels are called boltholes.   There are lots of boltholes in a mob's territory.

burrow   A hole in the ground where an animal lives.

mimic   Sometimes an animal can copy or mimic the behaviour of another animal to get food or to stay safe.

mob   A group of meerkats that lives together is called a mob.   It includes adults and pups.

predator   An animal that hunts and eats other animals is called a predator.

territory   An area where a particular animal makes its home.